The Dance of Love: A Poetic Tale of Love, Connection & Understanding

By Aaron Fields

Illustration: Amelia Alvin

Copyright © 2024 Aaron Fields. All rights reserved.

Published by The Write Perspective, LLC

Dallas, Texas,

All rights reserved. No part of this book shall be reproduced or transmitted in any form or by any means, electronic, mechanical, magnetic, photographic including photocopying, recording or by any information storage and retrieval system, without prior written permission of the publisher. No copyright liability is assumed with respect to the use of the information contained in this book. Even though every precaution has taken in preparation of this book, the publisher/author assumes no responsibility for errors or omissions. Neither is any liability assumed for any damage that results from the use of the information in this book.

ISBN: 978-1-953962-59-1

Dance & Love is a Beautiful Combination

Aaron Fields

In the rhythm of his steps, a love story unfolds,

His dance moves speak volumes, more precious than gold.

With each smile and graceful sway, he shows his love so true,

Creating a special bond that only their hearts knew.

His movements are a language, expressing care and grace

In his arms, she finds comfort, in his embrace.

Through the dance, he whispers words unspoken,

A connection so deep, their love is unbroken.

With every twirl and spin, she feels understood and completed,

His dance makes a safe space, she doesn't feel depleted.

With each step, he builds a bridge of trust,

A foundation of love, strong and not rushed.

In the dance, they create a world of their own,

Where love and appreciation are beautifully shown.

Through his moves, she feels a sense of security,

A dance of love, filled with joy and purity.

The Dance of Love represents a deep emotional connection and delicate balance in a romantic relationship. The Dance of Love can be viewed in a poetic way to describe how lovers interact with each other, responding to each other's needs and feelings.

From a cultural standpoint, The Dance of Love has cultural significance in many different societies. The Dance of Love can be viewed as a metaphor that resonates with human experience of love and connection.

In many different cultures, The Dance of Love can have various forms of meanings as well as reflect the diversity of love's expression around the globe.

I hope this book has given you a deeper understanding of this expression and its use.